WALKING CL

ROMSE

and the Test Valley

Number Seventy One in the popular series
of walking guides

Contents

Walked, Written and Drawn by Clive Brown

Published by Clive Brown
ISBN 978-1-907669-71-2

PLEASE
Take care of the countryside
Your leisure is someone's livelihood

Close gates
Start no fires
Keep away from livestock and animals
Do not stray from marked paths
Take litter home
Do not damage walls, hedgerows or fences
Cross only at stiles or gates
Protect plants, trees and wildlife
Keep dogs on leads
Respect crops, machinery and rural property
Do not contaminate water

Although not essential we recommend good walking boots; during hot weather take something to drink on the way. All walks can easily be negotiated by an averagely fit person. The routes have been recently walked and surveyed, changes can however occur, please follow any signed diversions. Some paths cross fields which are under cultivation. All distances and times are approximate.

The maps give an accurate portrayal of the area, but scale has however been sacrificed in some cases for the sake of clarity and to fit restrictions of page size.

Walking Close To have taken every care in the research and production of this guide but cannot be held responsible for the safety of anyone using them.

During very wet weather, parts of these walks may become impassable through flooding, check before starting out. Stiles and rights of way can get overgrown during the summer; folding secateurs are a useful addition to a walker's rucksack.

Thanks to Angela for help in production of these booklets

Views or comments?
walkingcloseto@yahoo.co.uk

71:A

Walking Close to Romsey and the Test Valley

Romsey Abbey was founded in 907AD by Elflaeda the granddaughter of Alfred the Great. The town grew up around the religious settlement. A Viking raid in 993 destroyed much of the abbey and town; it was rebuilt around 1000 and substantially rebuilt as a convent in the reign of King Stephen in the 12th century. Because the abbey was also used as a place of worship by the ordinary people of Romsey the building survived the reformation and was bought by the town for £100.

Florence Nightingale (1820-1910), the nursing heroine of the Crimean War, was born in her namesake city five years after the end of the Napoleonic Wars and died in London four years before the start of the First World War. Public opinion wanted to see her buried in Westminster Abbey, but she left instructions that she wished to be interred in the family tomb in East Wellow churchyard (walk no 4). Nearby Embly Park had been bought by her father in 1826.

The country house Broadlands sits on the banks of the River Test on the edge of Romsey. The estate had been bought in 1736 by Henry Temple who had become the 1st Viscount Palmerston in 1723. He rebuilt the house and employed Capability Brown to remodel the gardens and landscape the parkland. The 3rd Viscount (another Henry Temple) was Prime Minister twice, from 1855-1858 and from 1859 until his death in 1865. A statue of Palmerston stands in the Market Place at Romsey; he is the man who is reputed to have said on his deathbed "Die, my dear doctor. That is the last thing I shall do". He died childless so the title became extinct and Broadlands passed to his stepson William Cowper who added Temple to his surname. He also died without issue and the estate was inherited by his distant ancestor, Edwina Ashley.

In 1922, Edwina married Broadlands second famous resident, Earl Mountbatten. Their colourful life during the 20s and 30s was a marked contrast to their careers during the Second World War. She spent the war with the St John's Ambulance whilst the Earl started the war in command of HMS Kelly, which was sunk during the Battle of Crete and later he became Supreme Allied Commander in South East Asia. He was the last Viceroy of India in 1947, First Lord of the Admiralty from 1955-59 and Chief of the Defence Staff until 1965. After his murder by the IRA in 1979, he was buried in Romsey Abbey. The Mountbatten title unusually passed to the Earl's daughter Patricia (born 1924), who is the present Countess.

We feel that it would be difficult to get lost with the instructions and map in this booklet, but recommend carrying an Ordnance Survey map. Most of the walks are on Explorer Map No 131, walk no 5 is on the New Forest Outdoor Leisure Map no OL22 and walk no 6 is on the Winchester Map no 132; Landranger nos 184,185 and 196 cover at a smaller scale. Roads, geographical features and buildings, not on our map but visible from the walk can be easily identified.

1 Awbridge Danes Lake

$6^1/_2$ Miles $3^1/_4$ Hours

Use the small roadside parking area on the A3084 at Awbridge, close to the junction leading to Kimbridge. No facilities. The walk uses a narrow and busy section of road at Kimbridge; parts of the walk can also be very muddy in wet weather.

1 Leave out of the back past the Test Way marker post and follow the fenced path through the trees to the road. Turn right, carefully along this busy road to the signpost on the left at the level crossing. Step over and take this wide track left, straight over the crossroads of tracks and past the houses to the road.

2 Cross and go through the kissing gate opposite, follow the fenced path and go over the stile in the hedge at the top. Keep ahead across the field which may be under cultivation although a path should be visible within any crop. Cross the stile and go up the field edge with the trees to the left, carry on across the narrow neck of field and turn left with the fence and the trees to the right.

3 Go across the stile at the end and bear left and right on the field edge to the top left corner. Continue over the hill top and down, a track should be well marked, over the stile at the bottom and turn right, along the grass verge of this busy road for 120yds to the stile on the left. Cross and walk up to the next stile.

4 Turn left along the field edge with the hedge to the right for half a mile past Wood Farm to the kissing gate on the right. Go through and follow this fenced path through the trees and along the field edge with the fence to the right, to the road. Turn right, past the junction in Newtown to the signpost at the tarmac bridleway.

5 Turn left past the wide metal gate and up the path through the trees. Keep direction through the golf course to the road. Turn right for 160yds to the signpost on the left.

6 Take the narrow path left, through the trees and up the left hand field edge with Awbridge Danes Lake down to the left. At the crossroads of paths, turn right and cross the stile at the top. Continue into the field for 150yds and turn left through the wide metal gate, carry on up the wide hedged far road past Hilberry Farm to the road.

7 Turn left and almost immediate right at the signpost, up the narrow path and over the stile; turn left and cross the next stile. Keep direction downslope over the stile on the left and turn right, along the narrow path to the road. Take the road right to the signpost on the left.

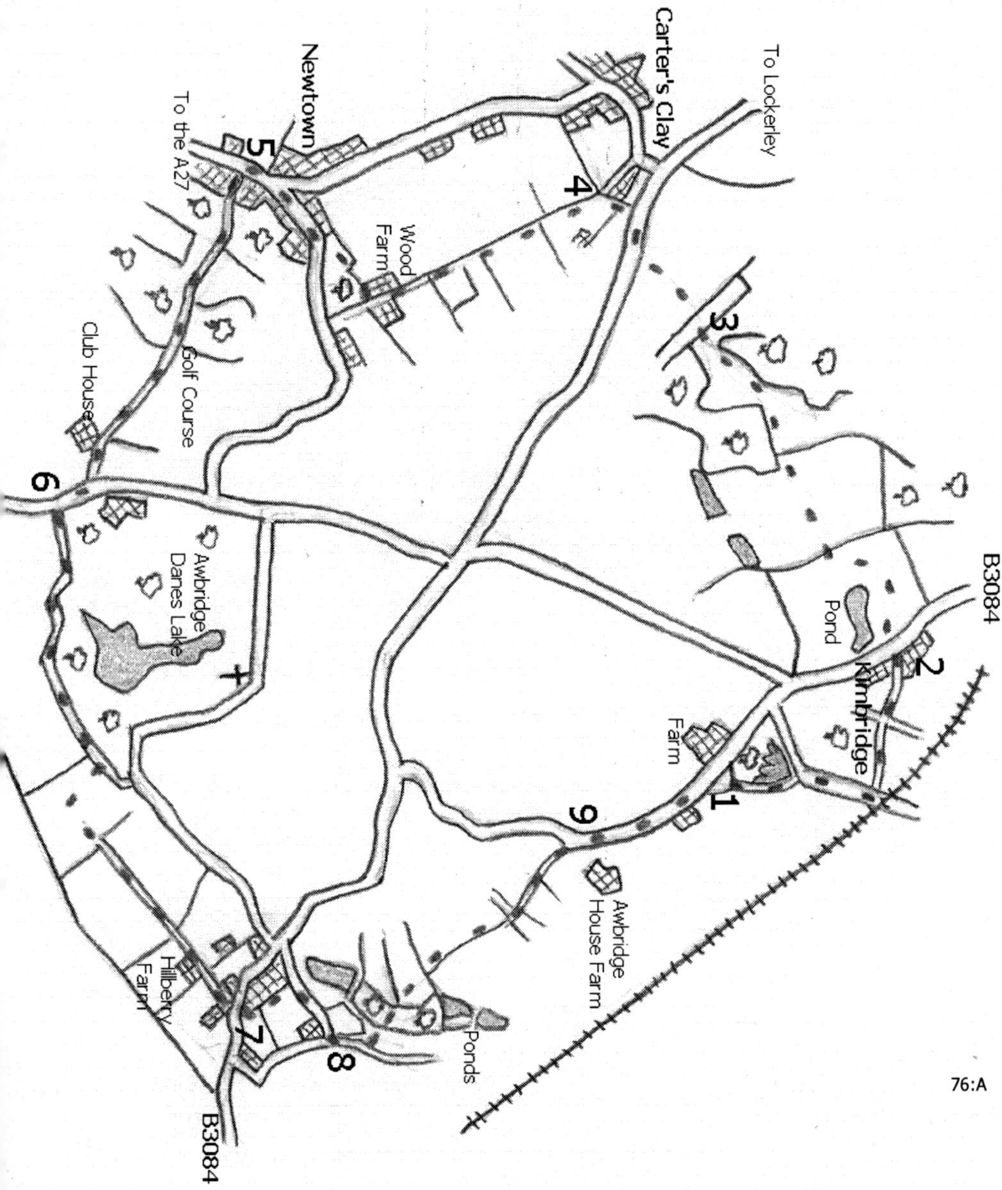

8 Go down the path through trees and step over the stile at the end, bear left across the footbridge in the trees and continue ahead along the boardwalk. Exit over the stile at the top and bear right along the track in the grass, over a footbridge/stile and the next stile. Follow the field edge to the kissing gate and keep direction along the narrower path to the road.

9 Keep ahead/right, along the grass verge of this busy road to the parking area and your vehicle.

2 Michelmersh

$7^1/_2$ Miles $3^3/_4$ Hours

Find a parking space in Braishfield; no toilets. Local pubs the 'Newport Arms' and the 'Wheatsheaf'.

1 Start from the war memorial; go down Dummers Road and fork left of the pond; keep right/straight on at the junction to the signpost at the metal gates. Take the narrow footpath left, all the way to the road.

2 Turn right, bearing left downslope over the junction to the signpost for Windmill Cottage and bear left up this track. Bear left at the cottage, follow this stony farm road to the signpost at the narrow hedged track and keep straight on. At the road turn right, bearing left to a signpost in the sharp corner.

3 Step over the stile and walk up this wide track between trees, through a dip to a junction of tracks at the corner of a wood. Turn left to the signpost at Manor Farm, take the farm road right, between farm buildings and bear right of the house at the fork. Follow the track left of the trees, just before it swings right, cross two stiles close together on the left.

4 Take the track through the trees and continue with the fence to the left, past a wide gate to the road. After 45yds, turn right at the signpost and keep direction along the track on the field edge to the marker post. Turn left through the gate, down the driveway to the road.

5 Continue straight on, right of the barn to the T-junction; turn right and almost immediate left at a footpath signpost, past a shed and along the edge of a garden. Carry on down the left hand field edge, through the gap at the bottom right and turn right down the path along the edge of the trees. Turn left at the end and follow this path left and right; go through the barriers and turn right, up to the road.

6 Turn left for 90yds to the signpost and turn right, through the hedge gap; cross the field ahead which may be under cultivation although a path should be well marked within any crop. Keep ahead through the trees, past green gates and carry on past a signpost to the road, turn left up to the signpost on the right.

7 Take the wide access road to the right and continue along the grass track between fences; follow the path left with the dyke to the right. Cross the stile at the end and bear right to the road right of the barns. Turn right, along this road bearing left at the junction to a stile where the road swings right.

Completed on the next Page (Eight)

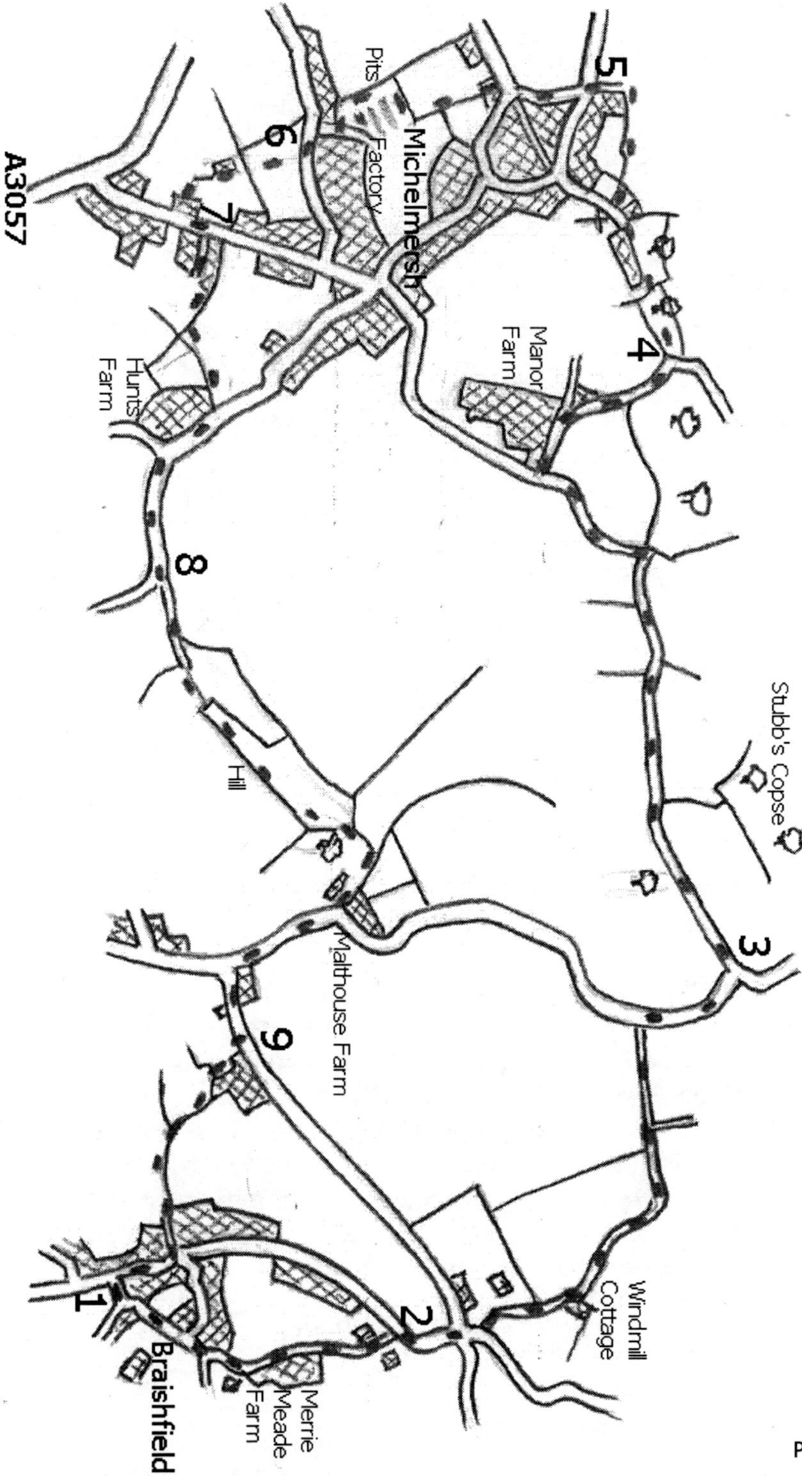

A3057
Michelmersh
Pits
Factory
Manor Farm
Hunts Farm
Stubb's Copse
Hill
Malthouse Farm
Windmill Cottage
Merrie Meade Farm
Braishfield
1
2
3
4
5
6
7
8
9

71:A

Completion of 2 Michelmersh from the previous Page

8 Step over the stile and keep direction along this wide track to a double signpost at the trees. Take the narrow left hand track through the trees, carry on over the hill with the fence to the right and down over the stile in the right hand corner at the end. Keep direction along the right hand field edge with the trees to the left and turn right with the fence and trees to the left, over the stile and down the narrow path to the road. Turn right, to the T-junction and take the road left past the derelict barn to the signpost and turn right, over the stile.

9 Follow the field edge left, to the top left corner; go through the trees, bear left then right, along a row of trees and keep ahead bearing left upslope past a signpost. Continue up the field edge with a fence now left leading through the edge of a garden and down a driveway to the road in Braishfield. Turn right, back to the starting point at the war memorial.

3 Parnholt Wood

$6^3/_4$ Miles $3^1/_4$ Hours

Find a parking space in King's Somborne, no toilets. Post office/shop, general store and pub the 'Crown Inn'.

1 Start from the church; walk away from the main road up Church Road, up the slope out of the village and fork left at the junction. Continue for a third of a mile to the right-of-way signpost on the right.

2 Take this wide stony track for two and a quarter miles to the staggered crossroads where the trees end on the left.

3 Follow the track left, past the metal barrier at the end to the signpost. Turn left along the path at the edge of the trees, the route continues through a hedged path and a track between open fields to a signpost at the road.

4 Turn left along this wide hedged path to a gate, turn right and continue through the trees, past the signpost at the crossroads to the signpost on the right.

5 Bear right on a narrower path, downslope through trees, carry on between the fence and the hedge. As the fence bears away to the left continue direction along the right hand field edge, all the way to the road at King's Somborne. Turn left, back to the main road and left back to the church.

71:A

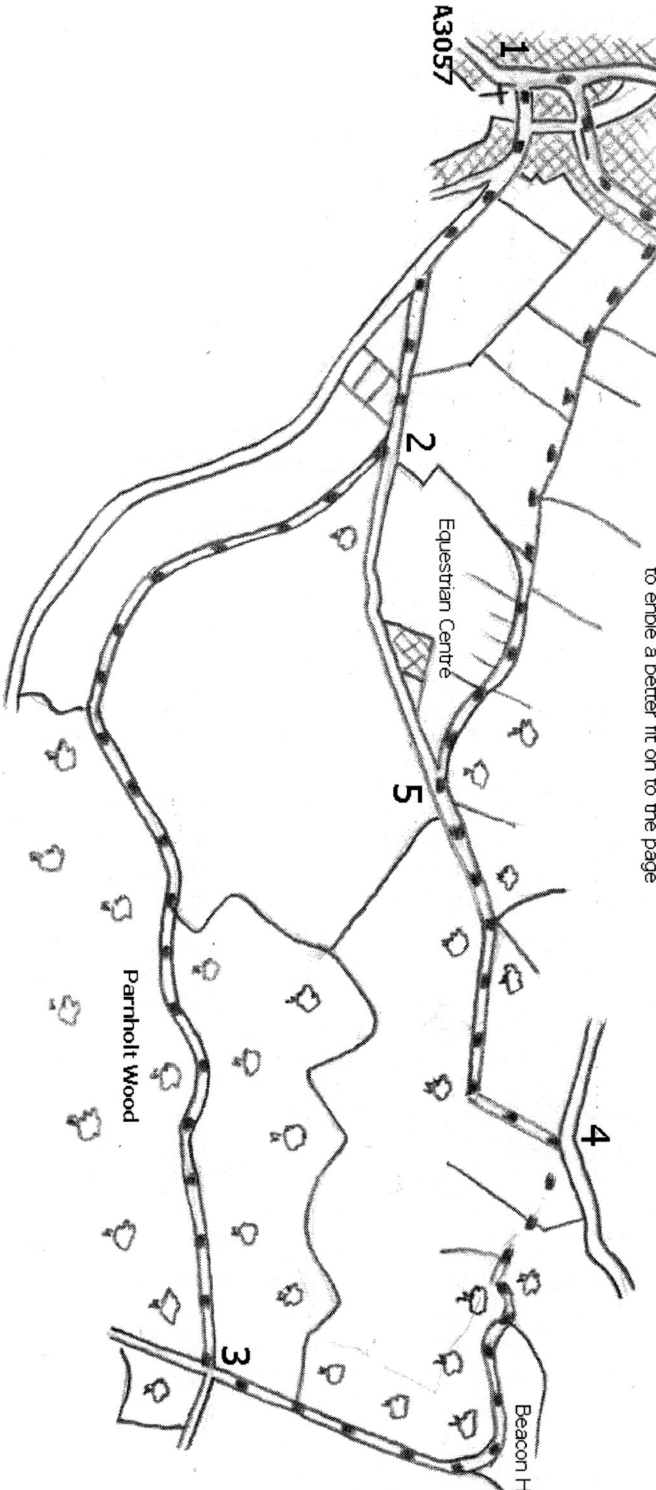

The map has been tilted slightly anti-clockwise to enble a better fit on to the page

4 Florence Nightingale

$6^1/_2$ Miles $3^1/_4$ Hours

Use the lay-by on the northern (eastbound) side of the A27, half a mile west of Sherfield English, 4 miles west of Romsey. No facilities.

1 Take the footpath west, straight over at the crossroads, to the signpost on the left. Turn left, through the gatehouse and follow the tarmac driveway.

2 Bear left/straight on at the fork and continue past Melchetcourt Farm bearing left and turn second right to the white house. Turn left along a wide farm road through trees and bear left to the signpost. Keep straight on upslope and carry on to the road at manor Farm.

3 Turn left, past the church to the T-junction and left up this surprisingly busy road to Pound Lane. Walk up the road to the junction and take the road right to the T-junction.

4 Turn left and immediate right, over the stile and up the left hand field edge with the trees to the left. Step over the midway stile and continue nearly to the corner. Turn left across the stile and follow the fenced path to the road.

5 Turn right and immediate left along the path with the wire fence to the left, through the kissing gate and over the footbridge in the trees. Continue along the path to the church, *the grave of Florence Nightingale is in the churchyard behind the church.* Carry on to the road.

6 Take the road left for 380yds to the signpost as the road swings right. Go over the stile and walk up the left hand field edge with the trees to the left to the stile on the left. Cross and keep ahead over the footbridge, bear right over the next footbridge. Continue to the road and turn left.

7 At the T-junction turn right and follow the road to the junction, go through the gate at the signpost left/ahead and bear left across the field which may be under cultivation although a track should be well marked within any crop. Join the path with the stream to the right, cross the stile and carry on along the right hand field edge to the road.

8 Turn right, to the A27 in Sherfield English, cross this busy road carefully and turn left along the roadside path to the lay-by and your vehicle.

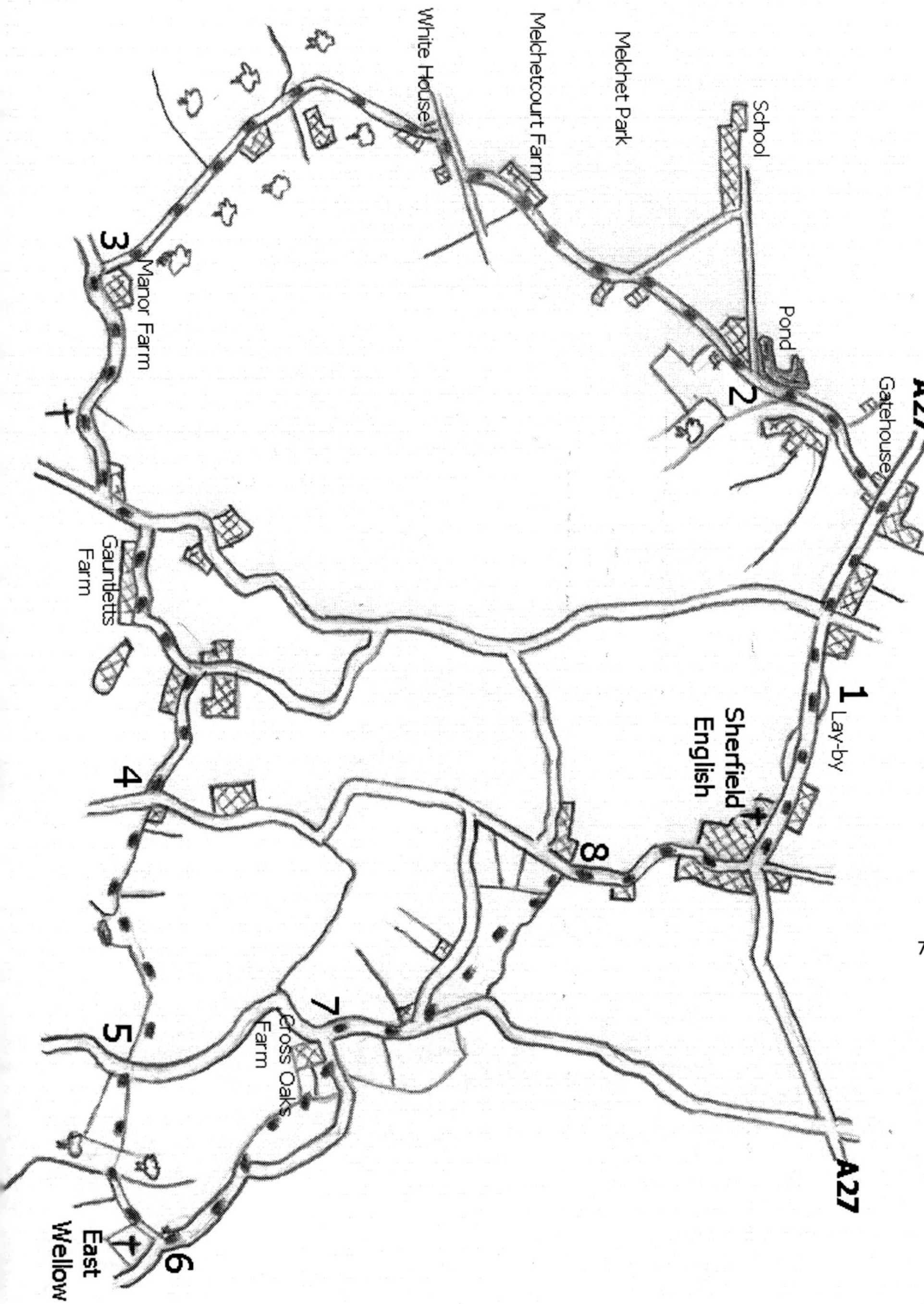
A27
Gatehouse
Pond
School
Melchet Park
Melchetcourt Farm
White House
Manor Farm
Gauntletts Farm
Sherfield English
Lay-by
Cross Oaks Farm
East Wellow
A27
1
2
3
4
5
6
7
8

71:A

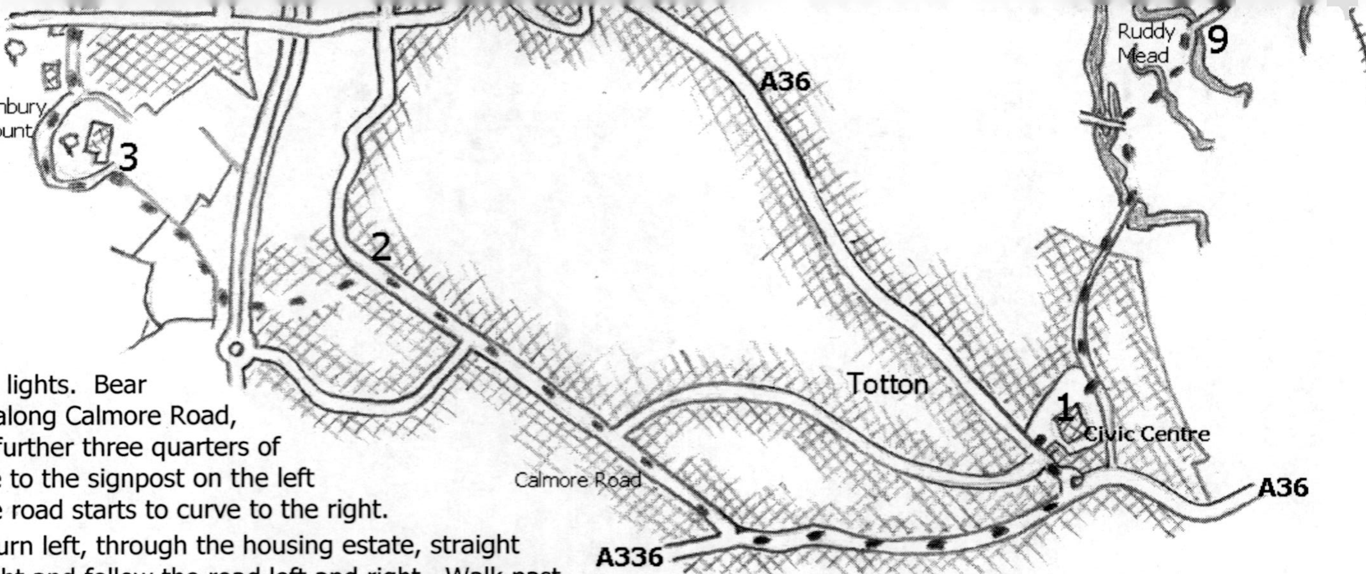

71:A

traffic lights. Bear right along Calmore Road, for a further three quarters of a mile to the signpost on the left as the road starts to curve to the right.

2 Turn left, through the housing estate, straight on/right and follow the road left and right. Walk past the barrier and along the narrow path between fences and trees; continue through the underpass beneath the A326. Bear right and fork right, parallel to the road; step over the stile and walk up the field edge with the hedge to the right. Carry on along the edge of the next field to the bottom of the slope.

3 Take the path left, upslope around Tatchbury Mount; past a marker post, right of the wooden fence to a metal gate between two yellow posts. Turn left along the wide track, straight on over the road and up the tree lined driveway. Continue all the way to the road and bear left to the T-junction.

Turn left, around the double bends and over Wade Bridge across the River Blackwater.

5 Take the farm driveway right, through Moorcourt Farm; bear left then turn right, past a wide metal gate. Follow this hardcore farm road bearing right at a confusing fork and on to the tarmac surface to a signpost at a sharp left hand corner. Turn left and carry on, bearing right, over the River Test at the bridge.

6 Turn immediate right at the signpost, along the wide track between hedges and keep direction on the lesser track with the trees to the left, to the T-junction

Completed on the next Page (Fourteen)

5 Ruddy Mead

$9^{3}/_{4}$ Miles $4^{3}/_{4}$ Hours

Use the car park at the Civic Centre, signposted from Salisbury Road, in Totton. Toilets close by; shops, restaurants and takeaways adjacent in the town.

1 Turn left along Salisbury Road to the roundabout and take the A336 (Ringwood Road) to the right, for two thirds of a mile to the

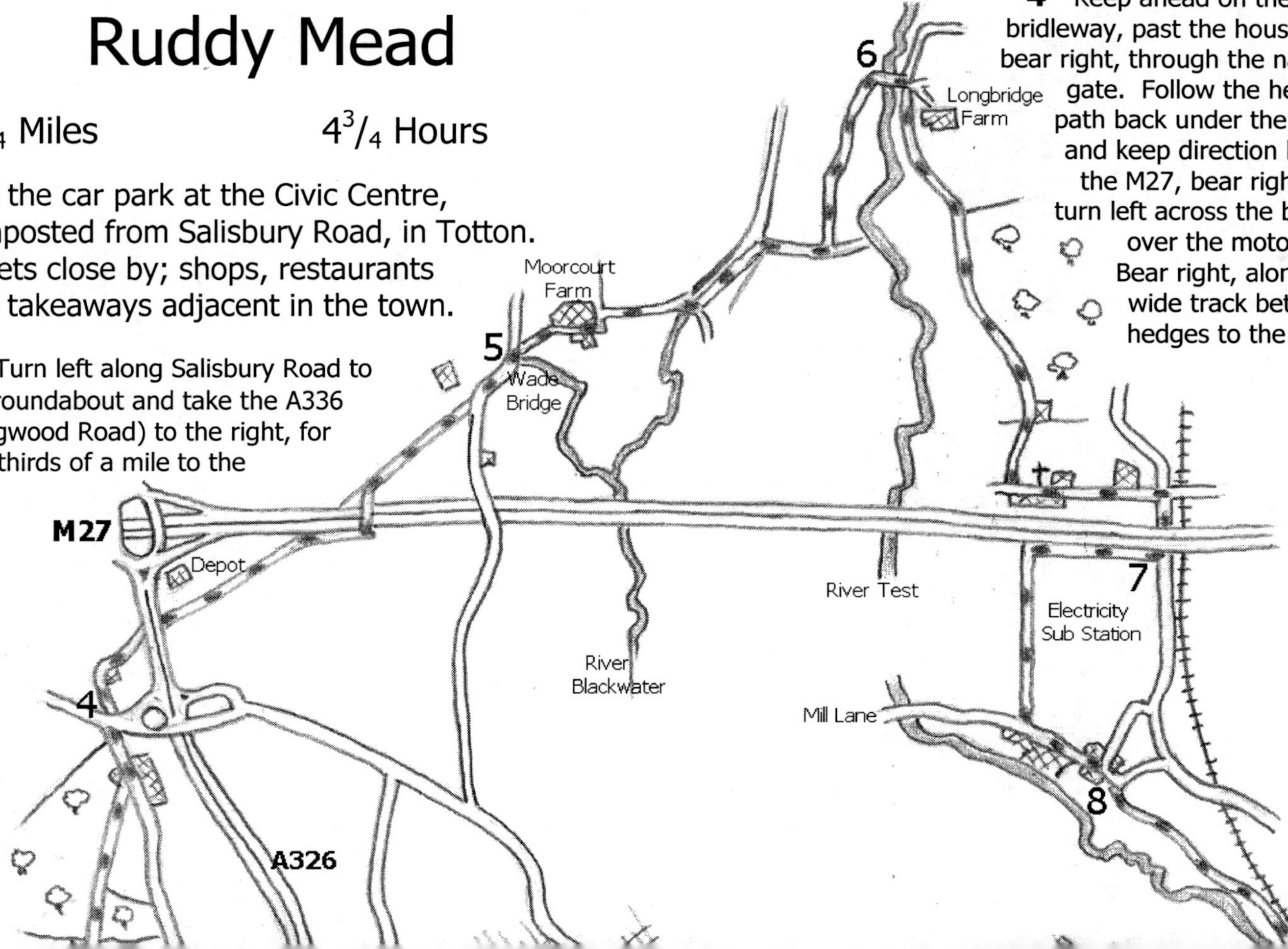

4 Keep ahead on the wide bridleway, past the house and bear right, through the narrow gate. Follow the hedged path back under the A326 and keep direction left to the M27, bear right and turn left across the bridge over the motorway. Bear right, along the wide track between hedges to the road.

Completion of 5 Ruddy Mead from the previous Page

with the road. Turn left, up to the crossroads and take the road right, under the M27.

7 At the signpost on the immediate right, turn right up the path parallel to the motorway; turn left with the path and continue to the road. Turn left, past the junction and over the white railed bridge to the signpost on the right.

8 Follow this path with the fence to the right, it runs parallel to the railway for 360yds and goes through a kissing gate. Turn right and cross the footbridge, carry on ahead and turn left over a wider bridge. Go past the metal gate and up the right hand field edge with the trees to the right; continue over the less substantial footbridge near the pylons.

9 Turn left along the boardwalk with Ruddy Mead to the right. Keep on this boardwalk as it meanders across the marsh and go through the gate to the hardcore track. Turn left along this wide tree lined bridleway and turn right, across the river. Keep ahead/left along the road in Totton bearing slight left and cut through to the right, to find the Civic Centre car park and your vehicle.

---

6 Farley Mount

$5^1/_2$ Miles $2^1/_2$ Hours

Use the parking area in Crab Wood local nature reserve on a minor road east of Winchester; Grid reference: SU433293, no facilities.

1 Turn left from the car park entrance along the path parallel to the road, join the road ahead and go straight on at the crossroads, upslope to the junction. Bear left, past the cul-de-sac sign, to the bridleway on the left marked by blue discs.

2 Turn left along this track for two thirds of a mile to the Ham Green information board. Take the path left, all the way to the road.

3 Turn right for 250yds to the T-junction and take the road left to Newbarn Farm. Continue through the farmyard and follow the hardcore farm road ahead for three quarters of a mile to the narrow gap on the left marked by a red disc.

4 Turn left along the fenced track through the field and keep direction on the wide track through the trees to the other side.

5 Take the path left, with the trees to the left and open ground on the right. Keep left on the path along the edge of the trees and continue up the path parallel to the road, back to the car park and your vehicle.

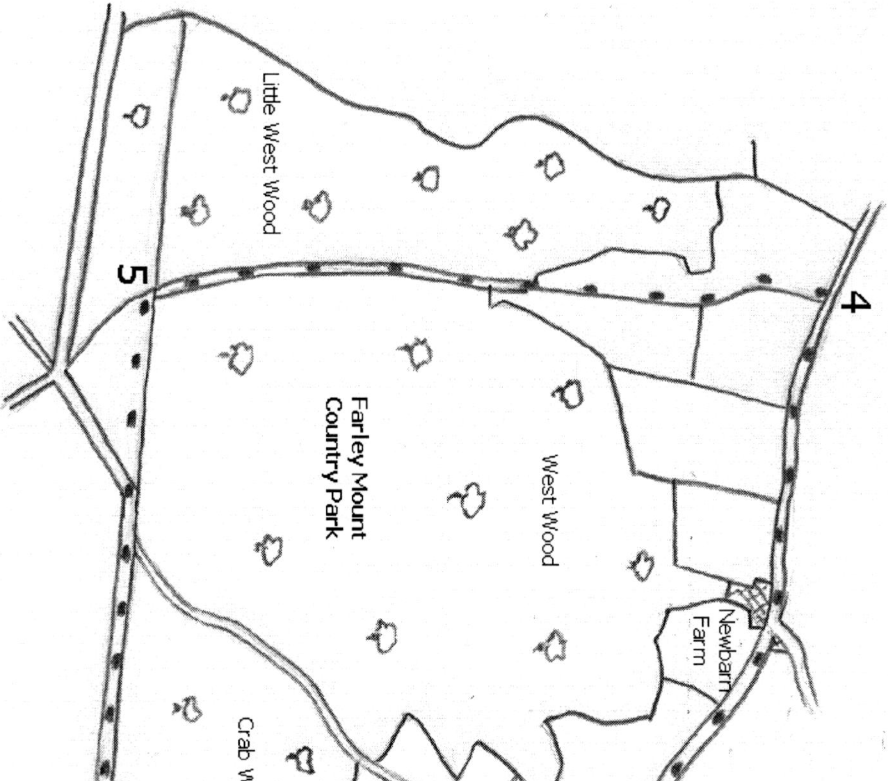
Little West Wood
5
4
Farley Mount
Country Park
West Wood
Newbarn
Farm
Crab Wood
1
Car
Park
To Sparsholt
3
2

71:A

7 Oakley Stream

5 Miles $2^1/_2$ Hours

Park in the nearside lay-by on the A3057 just north of the 'Bear and Ragged Staff' two miles north of Romsey.

1 Go back to the junction and turn left up Staff Road for two thirds of a mile to the junction and turn left to the next junction. Cross the road, go through the double gates, up the drive and exit through the narrow gate.

2 Keep direction through the dip and take the path ahead through the trees, past a marker post and through the narrow metal gate. Bear left past the left hand corner of the trees and further left through a kissing gate at a signpost. Descend the steep, handrailed slope and bear right, over the field to the road.

3 Cross carefully and go through the barrier opposite, continue across the tarmac driveway and the bridge over the River Test. Bear left over the stile at the wooden gate, keep ahead across the field and step over the stile/footbridge in the hedge. Turn left along the drive and cross the bridge over Oakley Stream, to the almost hidden kissing gate on the left. Follow this path between fences, back upslope to the road north of Mottisfont village.

4 Turn left, through the village, follow the road left and turn left at the sharper bend at the signpost. Turn right, into Church Lane, through the churchyard and out of the gate at the back; turn left and immediate right, up the wide hedged track. Go through the metal gate and follow the path through the field, continue over the footbridge and upslope through the trees.

5 Cross the bridge over the railway and carry on slight left to a crossroads of tracks. Take the track left to the road close to the level crossing; carefully follow this road left back to the A3057, the lay-by and your vehicle.

In its upper reaches the River Test is a chalk stream with an enviable reputation for the quality of its fly fishing for trout. Rain from the surrounding countryside soaks into the porous chalk under the soil. Water emerges from springs at a steady flow and a fairly constant temperature of 50° Fahrenheit. These conditions make it ideal for trout, salmon and grayling. The river's source is at the village of Ashe in Hampshire, east of Basingstoke. It flows for 40 miles, through Romsey to join the River Itchen and form Southampton Water.

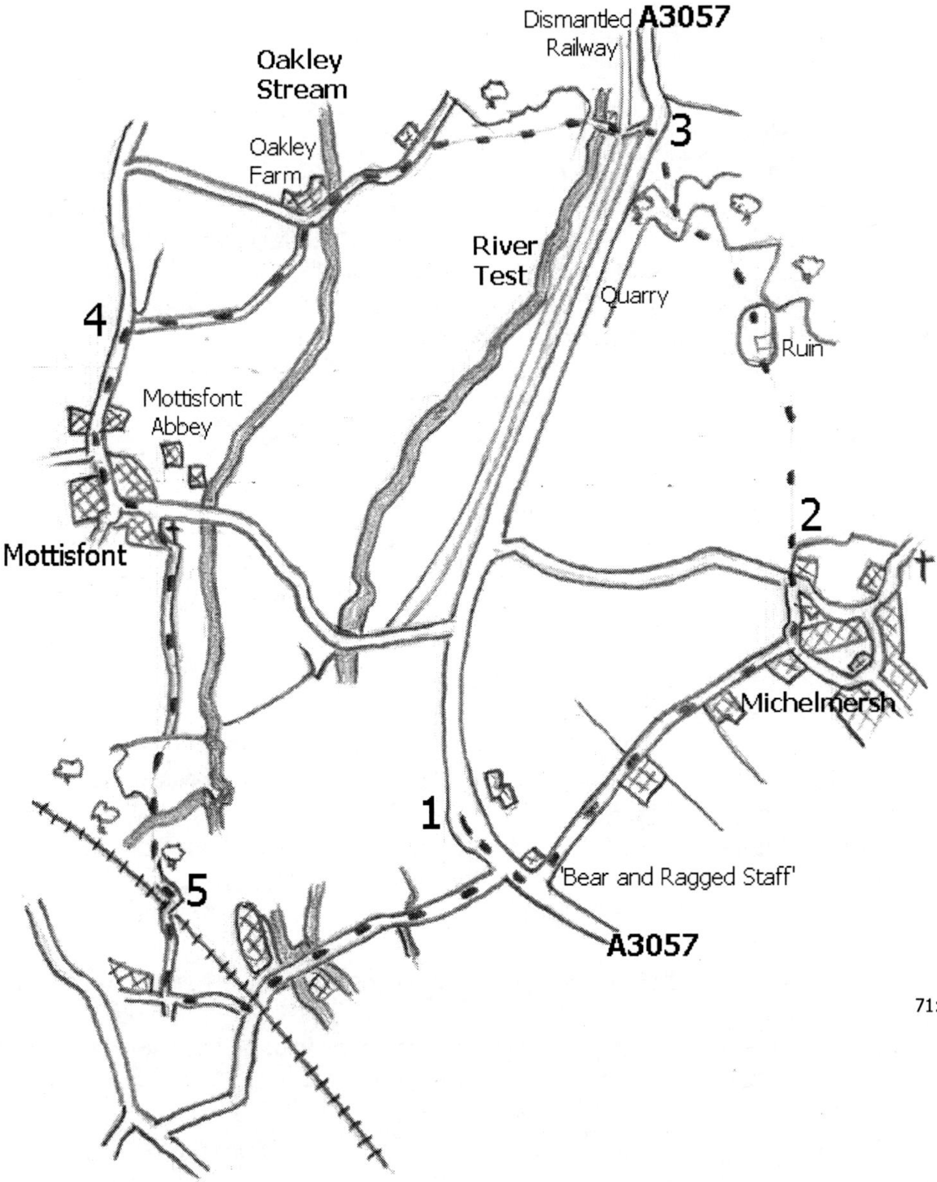
Dismantled Railway
A3057
Oakley Stream
Oakley Farm
3
River Test
Quarry
Ruin
4
Mottisfont Abbey
Mottisfont
2
Michelmersh
1
'Bear and Ragged Staff'
5
A3057

71:A

8 Red Gate

$6^1/_2$ Miles 3 Hours

There is sometimes space to park at the entrance to Ampfield Wood on the minor road between the A3090 and the A3057; no facilities. There could also be room in the small lay-by at the junction with the A3090. A start may also be made from Braishfield village, where the route goes through the 'Wheatsheaf' car park. The walk goes along a narrow minor road during point **4**.

1 Walk away from the road up the wide hardcore track between trees, past the first junction at a marker post to the marker post at the T-junction at the end.

2 Turn sharp left to the stile, step over and take the narrow fenced path to the right. Go through the tall kissing gate, turn left along the top of the slope and exit through the kissing gate here; cross the footbridge and go down the field edge with the trees to the left. At the bottom bear left on a wide track to a footbridge/stile; cross and bear left over the field to a kissing gate. (Do not go through).

3 Turn right, along the field edge with the fence to the left, go over the stile at the end and through the adjacent kissing gate. Continue through the car park of the 'Wheatsheaf' to the road.

4 Turn right and bear right, into Common Hill Road; follow the road bearing right at the junction, through Pucknall and past the junction at Lower Slackstead, to the bridleway signpost on the right just past Bells Ground.

5 Take the wide hardcore bridleway back into Ampfield Wood; keep ahead at the junctions and continue on this main track to the wooden gate at the end. Turn right, through Knapp around the double bend, to the wide unmarked track on the right.

6 Turn right, through the tree nursery, to the signpost; turn left and almost immediate right past a signpost. Keep direction, through the gate and downslope into Ampfield Wood again, carry on over the crossroads with a wider hardcore forest road, to a T-junction with a wider track. Turn left to a signpost and right to Red Gate, the entry point on this side of the wood.

7 Take the track left, past a wooden barrier, upslope between trees to the junction passed earlier at point **2**. Turn left, along the wide forest road to the starting point.

The Rev W Awdry (1911-1997), author of the 'Thomas the Tank Engine' children's books was born at the vicarage in Ampfield.

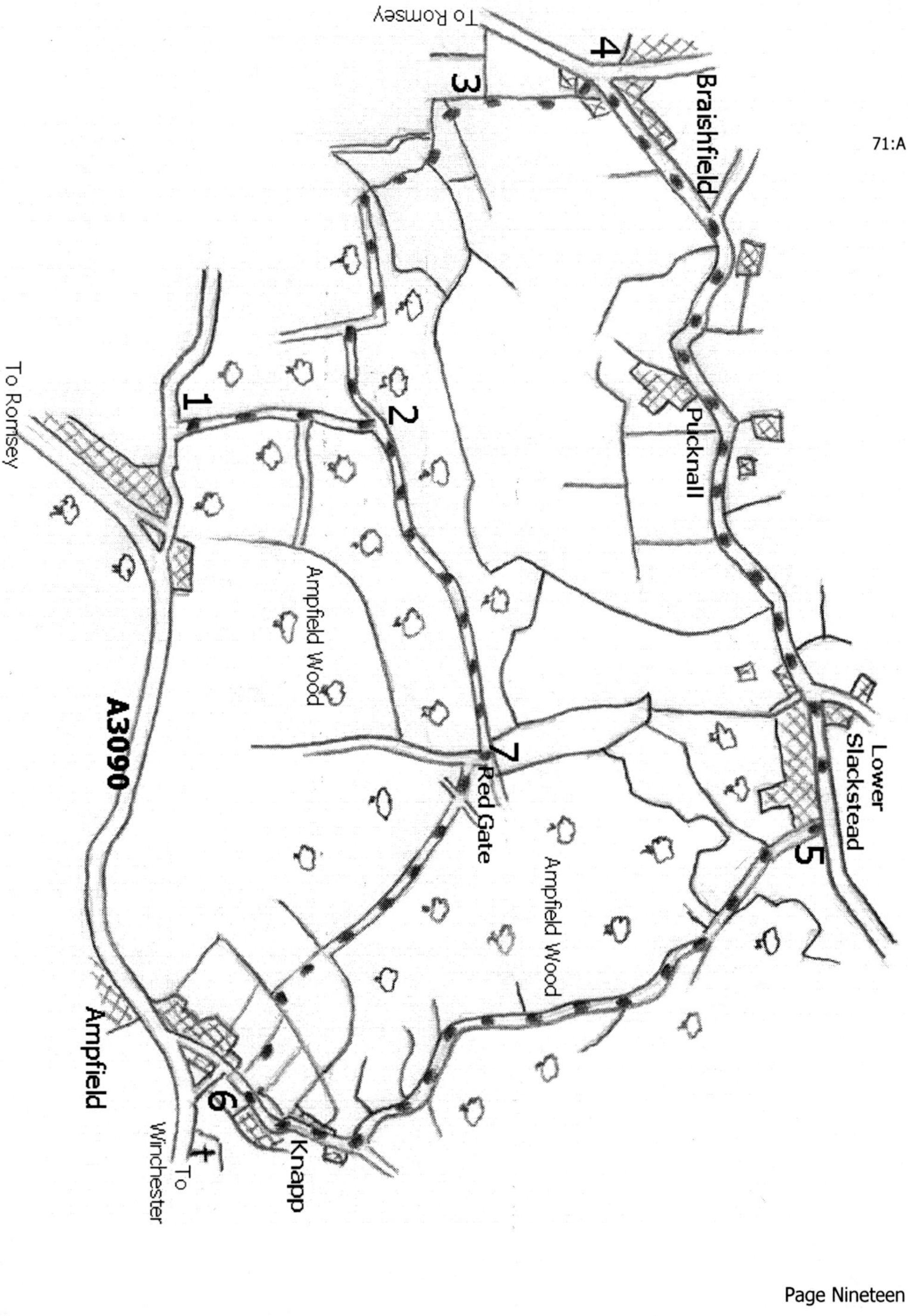
To Romsey
4
3
Braishfield
Pucknall
1
2
To Romsey
Ampfield Wood
A3090
7
Red Gate
Lower
Slackstead
5
Ampfield Wood
Ampfield
6
Knapp
To
Winchester

9 Tote Hill

$4^3/_4$ Miles $2^1/_4$ Hours

Find a parking space in Newtown, north of the A27, east of Romsey. Grid ref SU309237. No facilities.

1 Start from the central junction and take the road towards Carter's Clay to the footpath signpost on the left. Step over the stile and walk up the left hand field edge with the hedge to the left, through the gate in the corner. Turn right, up the narrow path between fences; continue up the left hand field edge, through the dip and along the narrow path between the fence and the trees, passing left of the house up the driveway to the road at Tote Hill.

2 Cross and go past the footpath signpost, through the trees and join the road straight on to the stile at the signpost on the left. Go over and walk up the left hand field edge with the hedge to the left, continue into the narrow strip between trees and across the stile at the end. Bear right, along the short length of right hand field edge, through the narrow belt of trees and over the stile.

3 Bear left across this field to the far left corner, over the stile and follow the path right, through the trees and the dip. Keep ahead on the narrow path, over the stile and up the field edge with the hedge to the right. At and unmarked point keep straight on upslope, this field may be under cultivation although a track should be well marked within any crop, to the stiles at the top, right of Painshill Farm.

4 Cross both stiles and follow the left hand field edge to the stile on the left, cross this stile, the field and the stile ahead. Turn right along the concrete farm road, down to the T-junction and turn left, upslope to the stile on the left at the top.

5 Step over and continue along the right hand field edge to the far right corner. Keep direction with the hedge now left for just over a third of a mile, through a gap on to the wide track and bear right between the hedge and the trees passing left of the houses. Continue past Gambledown Farm, past a reverse fork, along the tarmac drive to the T-junction at the road.

6 Turn left towards Tote Hill for 190yds to the signpost and take the narrow path through the trees to the marker post at the end. Turn left to the next marker post at a diversion; turn left along the path between the fence and the trees. Keep direction along paths and field edges to the road in Newtown to find your vehicle.

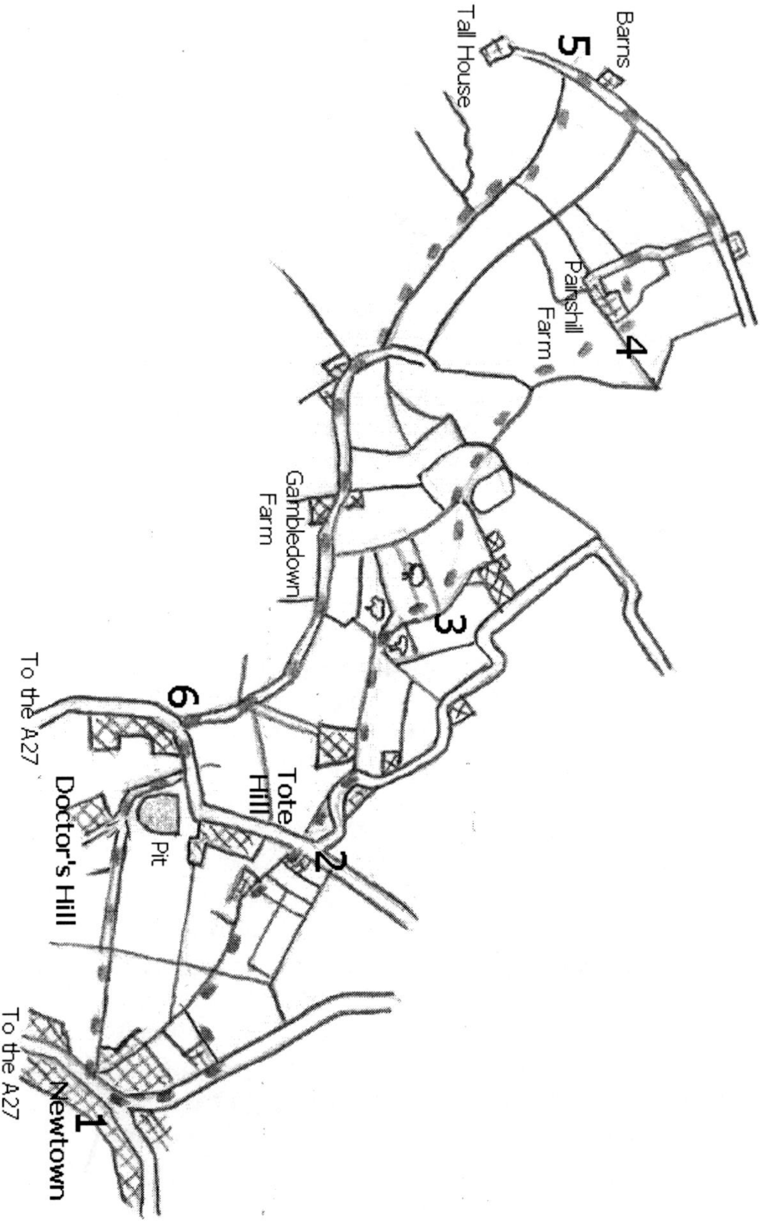
Barns
5
Tall House
Painshill Farm
4
Gambledown Farm
3
To the A27
6
Tote Hill
Doctor's Hill
Pit
2
To the A27
1
Newtown

71:A

10 Mottisfont Abbey

$3^3/_4$ Miles $1^3/_4$ Hours

Use the parking area at Spearywell Wood (National Trust sign), grid reference SU316278, off the B3084 north of Spearywell. No facilities.

1 Turn right, from the car park entrance, along the surprisingly busy road to the signpost on the left and turn left, past the metal gate. Bear slight right across this field which may be under cultivation although a path should be well marked within any crop, to the far corner. Go through the wide gap and keep direction still, to the bottom right, join the road and turn left to the T-junction.

2 Take the road right, through Mottisfont village to the corner and turn right, up Hatt Lane for 270yds to the signpost on the left. Turn left and bear right, through the hedge, cross the field ahead, which may be under cultivation but should have a visible path, to the far corner. Pass through the kissing gate and continue down to the road.

3 Keep straight on between hedges and cross this busy railway line with great care. Follow the right hand field edge with the hedge to the right and bear right with the gravelly driveway through the metal kissing gate left of the cottage. Carry on between trees with the stream to the left; the path widens out and goes through a wide gateway. The path goes along the field edge with a barbed wire fence to the right, through a narrow gate and over a footbridge/stile. Continue over two more footbridges and bear slight left to the kissing gate in the corner.

4 Turn right, up the path between hedges, back under the railway and up the fenced path. Bear left with the path, past the National Trust signpost and up a short length of path between trees, through the derelict kissing gate. Cross the field ahead a path should be well marked, over the footbridge and follow the trail bearing right through trees again, to a signpost at a staggered crossroads of tracks.

5 Turn right, along the wide track between trees; carry on past the gate at Cadbury Farm and keep ahead down this stony track to the road. Take the road left, back to the car park to find your vehicle.

The Abbey at Mottisfont was founded in 1201 for pilgrims to worship the relic purporting to be the finger of St John the Baptist. At the reformation it passed to Sir William Sandys who converted the existing nave into his country home and added two new wings. The estate is now part of the National Trust.

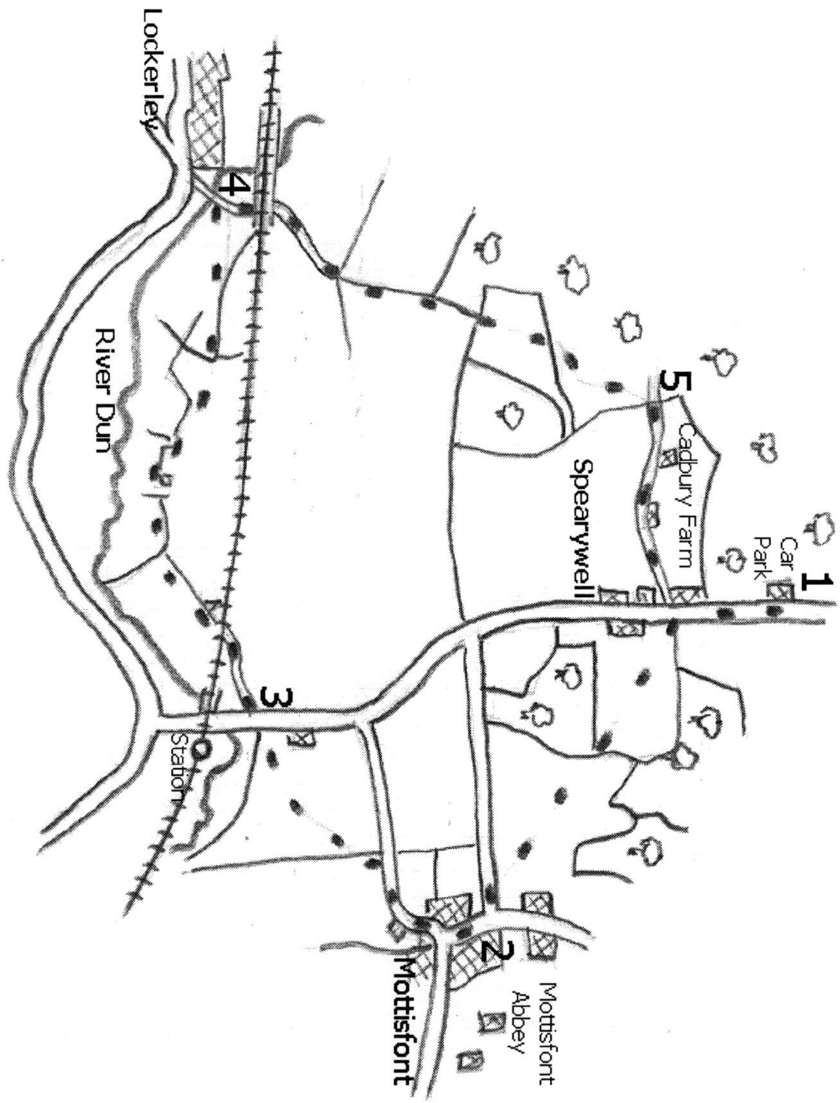
Lockerley
4
River Dun
5
Cadbury Farm
Spearywell
Car Park
1
3
Station
2
Mottisfont
Mottisfont Abbey

The 'Walking Close to' Series

Peterborough
The Nene near Peterborough
The Nene Valley Railway near Wansford
The Nene near Oundle
The Torpel Way (Peterborough to Stamford)
The Great North Road near Stilton

Cambridge
Grafham Water (Huntingdonshire)
The Great Ouse in Huntingdonshire
The Cam and the Granta near Cambridge
Newmarket
The Isle of Ely

Northamptonshire/Warwickshire
The Nene near Thrapston
The Nene near Wellingborough
The River Ise near Kettering
The Nene near Northampton
Pitsford Water
Rockingham Forest
Daventry and North West Northamptonshire
Rugby
Stratford-upon-Avon (Late Spring 2013)

Leicestershire
Rutland Water
Eye Brook near Uppingham
The Soar near Leicester
Lutterworth
The Vale of Belvoir (North Leicestershire)
Melton Mowbray
The Welland near Market Harborough

Bedfordshire/Milton Keynes
The Great Ouse near Bedford
The Great Ouse north of Milton Keynes
Woburn Abbey

Suffolk
Lavenham in Suffolk
Bury St Edmunds
The Stour near Sudbury
The Orwell near Ipswich
Dedham Vale
Stowmarket
Clare, Cavendish and Haverhill
Southwold and the Suffolk Coast
Aldeburgh, Snape and Thorpeness

Hampshire
Romsey and the Test Valley

Essex/Hertfordshire
Hertford and the Lee Valley
The Colne near Colchester
Epping Forest (North London)
Chelmsford

Wiltshire/Bath
The Avon near Bath
Bradford-on-Avon
Corsham and Box
The Avon near Chippenham

Lincolnshire
The Welland near Stamford
Bourne and the Deepings
South Lincolnshire
The Lincolnshire Wolds (South)
The Lincolnshire Wolds (North)

Somerset, Devon & Dorset
Cheddar Gorge
Glastonbury and the City of Wells
The Quantock Hills
The East Devon Coast (Sidmouth, Branscombe and Beer)
Exmouth and East Devon
Blandford Forum (Dorset)
Shaftesbury and Gillingham (Dorset)

Norfolk
The Norfolk Broads (Northern Area)
The Norfolk Broads (Southern Area)
The Great Ouse near King's Lynn
North West Norfolk (Hunstanton and Wells)
Thetford Forest
North Norfolk (Cromer and Sheringham)

Nottinghamshire
Sherwood Forest
The Dukeries (Sherwood Forest)
The Trent near Nottingham

Oxfordshire/Berkshire
The Thames near Oxford
The Cotswolds near Witney
The Vale of White Horse
Woodstock and Blenheim Palace
Henley-on-Thames
Banbury
The River Pang (Reading/Newbury)
The Kennet near Newbury

Cumbria
Cartmel and Southern Lakeland

Hereford and Worcester
The Severn near Worcester
South West Herefordshire (Hay-on-Wye and Kington)
The Malvern Hills